YOU ARE
GOD'S GIFT
TO JESUS

JOEL HESCH

Published and printed in the US by Goshen Press, Lynchburg, VA.

Details in stories or anecdotes have been changed to protect the identities of the persons involved.

Interior and Cover Design: 1106 Design

ISBN: 978-1-940011-07-3 hardcover
ISBN: 978-1-940011-08-0 softcover
ISBN: 978-1-940011-09-7 eBooks

Christian Life/Inspirational

Table of Contents

Chapter 1

Gift of the Circle of Life

LIFE IS ALL ABOUT GIFTS. That's why we love giving and receiving gifts so much. Most people don't realize that the reason gifts are so enjoyable is because gift giving was designed by God to give meaning and fulfillment to life.

In this book you'll discover that there are five primary gifts built into every human, and we aren't fulfilled unless we appreciate and embrace each one. These gifts are intertwined and complete the circle of life.

The next chapter begins with the First Gift, which is you. Although life will always remain somewhat of a mystery, God the Father provides us with some insight by revealing that, out of the purest act of love, He purposefully created you so that you could be given as a precious gift to His beloved son, Jesus. What great joy the Father had in not only creating you in the image of Jesus, but also presenting you to Him as a present. There is no greater present God the Father could have given to Jesus than you. That also explains the great joy Jesus had in receiving you as a gift. In fact, the next three gifts flow from the boundless love Jesus has for you, His most prized and precious gift.

That brings us to the Second Gift. It's the gift of the precious names Jesus selected for you. Many of these names you may have never heard of before. What's so special about them is that these names not only signify your great worth to Jesus, but, by giving these names to you, God also instilled deep inside your soul a longing to live out your new names. You'll feel this urge more and more as your life increasingly reflects the love and character of Jesus. Here are just a few of your new names that you'll learn about in this book: *Dearly Loved, Ambassador of Christ,* and *Chosen by God.* Come try on your many new names; they'll make a perfect fit.

The Third Gift is the precious promises Jesus makes to you. One of the most recognized promises is that Jesus will never leave or forsake you, no matter what you do. That means even if you turn your back on Jesus, He will never let you go, and will always lovingly call you back to His side and protect you throughout the ages. Many of His promises are well-known, but this book will reveal the many hidden promises that are waiting for you. These promises are sure to become your new and trusted friends.

The Fourth Gift is Jesus actually giving Himself to you. You may have heard a sermon at church on Sunday morning, preaching that Jesus loves you so much that He laid down His life for you. With this book, you'll go on a journey down the little-known side streets to get a fresh, unique understanding of the greatness of the love Jesus has for you. You'll learn how and why He gave — and keeps giving — His life specifically for you and to you. Plan to have your heart opened as the mystery of the divine union being offered to you is revealed.

The Fifth Gift is different from the rest, but is necessary to complete the circle. The first four are gifts from God to you. The final gift is the one you give. It's where you pay it forward by giving back your love to God and sharing your love with the world. Once you grasp and enjoy the first four gifts, the final one becomes almost automatic, because your heart and soul long to be a gift giver, like God the Father and Jesus, the ultimate gift givers. The circle of life will be fully connected as the joy of gift giving becomes your new and permanent nature.

Let's begin the journey to explore in greater detail these Five Gifts of life.

At the end of each Chapter, there will be a letter or modern-day psalm to God as an act of prayer and thanksgiving. May they touch your soul and lead you to writing your own.

Modern-Day Psalm: Lord, there is none like you.

Only you can fill my heart.

Lord, there is none like you. Oh, how my soul does thirst for you.

I look to the heavens to see you in your dwelling place.
I long to sit at your feet and offer you my praise.

Draw me to your side, and call out my name.
Consume me completely.

Lord, there is none like you.

Nothing else can satisfy. So, turn my thoughts toward you, and open my eyes to your splendor.

Lord, there is none like you.

I call out your name and seek your face.
Turn to me now. Reach out your hand.

Join my spirit with yours.
Grant me divine fellowship, and help me fulfill my purpose in life.

Oh, to know and love you, Lord — that is my
one true request.
Open my heart to you, my Lord and my God,
that I might possess you, for there is none like
you.

Chapter 2

Gift of You

Precious Gifts

Early on Christmas morning, Jenny's mom called out, "Honey, come quick … Santa's been here. There's a present with your name on it!"

Jenny's feet barely touched the floor as she raced from her room. Her eyes grew wide when she saw a huge package next to the tree. It had been carefully wrapped in gold foil, with a purple bow on top.

Jenny shouted, "I wonder what it could be?!"

"Go ahead, open it, and find out," her mom grinned.

Jenny's heart raced as she untied the bow. Holding her breath, she tore off the gold wrapper. Peering deep inside the box, she saw two big brown eyes looking back at her.

"A puppy?! Thank you, thank you, thank you! Oh, I love you, mommy! I will give her a special name and take real good care of her!"

Jenny's joy was obvious. She felt valued, loved, and even treasured.

Who received more joy — Jenny or her mom? It's too close to call.

By giving this gift, Jenny's mom showed the great depths of her love. This particular gift had taken a lot of time and thought. Jenny's mom had nearly danced with anticipation as she selected just the right puppy for Jenny, anticipating the delight on her beloved daughter's face.

Her joy in giving this particular gift was so great that it far outweighed the costs, which included not only a hundred dollars in pet supplies, but also the time she would have to spend helping with walks, cleaning up messes, and doing everything that went along with giving a child a puppy. But, it was worth it!

You're That Gift!

Gift giving has always been a great source of joy. The first time gifts appeared in the New Testament was when three wise men traveled halfway around the world to bring gifts of gold, frankincense, and myrrh to the baby Jesus as He lay in the manger.[1] These three kings were filled with exceeding joy and keen anticipation as they trekked thousands of miles just to kneel before the Christ-child and present their most valuable gifts.

Did you know that God the Father once gave a special gift to His son, Jesus?

Imagine the God of the entire universe selecting a gift for his Son. He could create anything, even things unknown or unseen. It would be far beyond what we could afford or even imagine.

Of everything in the universe that God could give to Jesus, He chose something very special: You.

God the Father gave you as a gift to Jesus!

If we could have listened in on that moment when God the Father hand-selected you as a priceless gift to Jesus, we might have heard something like this:

"Son, you know that I love you?"

"Yes, Father, you have always shown me your great love. I have never doubted your love. I feel secure in your love."

"Son, you have pleased me greatly and I have picked out the perfect gift for you."

"My Father, whom I love, I will treasure whatever gift you give me."

---

[1] Matthew 2:11.

"Son, with all my love, I give to you … *(imagine Him saying your name).*"

"A human?! Thank you, thank you, thank you! Oh, I love you, Father! I will give my human a special name and take real good care of him!"

Who received more joy — Jesus, the gift receiver or God the Father, the gift giver? It's too close to call.

How do we know that's what happened? The Bible tells us so. Jesus mentions receiving you as a gift from the Father not once, but four times, just in the Book of John:

> All those **the Father gives me** will come to me.[2]

> **My Father, who has given them to me**, is greater than all; no one can snatch them out of my Father's hand.[3]

> I have revealed you to **those whom you gave me** out of the world. **They were yours; you gave them to me** and they have obeyed your word.[4]

> Father, I want those **you have given me** to be with me where I am, and to see my glory,

---

[2] John 6:37.
[3] John 10:27–29.
[4] John 17:6.

the glory you have given me because you
loved me before the creation of the world.[5]

Yes, God the Father personally gave *you* as a gift to
Jesus.

And, Jesus gladly received you as a gift. In fact, there
was a party in heaven that day, and all of the angels
rejoiced when Christ received you into His family.[6]

Let that sink in.

Picture a big bow on your chest and God the Father
smiling as He hands you to Christ as a gift.

Picture Christ cherishing you. In fact, we have the
promise of Jesus that He will never drive you away, but
protect you and keep you safe:

> I give them eternal life, and they shall never
> perish; no one will snatch them out of my
> hand.[7]

God the Father, the King of the Universe, promises
that no one can take you away from Jesus, and Jesus also
promises that no one will snatch you away from Him.
Now, *that* is security!

---

[5] John 17:24.
[6] Luke 15:10 ("In the same way, I tell you, there is rejoicing in the presence of the angels of God over one sinner who repents.")
[7] John 10:28.

Even if you don't feel worthy, you're still the precious gift the Father gladly gave to His son Jesus — who was thrilled to receive you.

Many movies have tried to capture the essence of this mystery with stories where an ordinary person wakes up one day to find out that they are a relative of a noble family, and are in line to become king or queen. At first, it's overwhelming, and doubts creep in. It even takes time to get used to it. But, once they are treated as a part of the royal family, they start believing it, and enjoying the benefits and privileges.

The Lord's gifts and promises, however, are not fables or make-believe, but the real thing. And, they're available to you, no matter what. No matter what humble roots you were born with. No matter how unworthy you feel. No matter what sins you've committed.

All of us were once living a self-focused life, and none of us were fit for His kingdom. But, despite your darkest secrets, God chose you as a gift, and Jesus adopted you as a son or daughter, and made you a permanent heir to the kingdom. In essence, you're a prince or princess forever.

Start believing it. Reject Satan's doubts and lies. The Devil wants to take away your joy. He would love to see you renounce your heavenly position.

A child may lovingly give her puppy a sparkling name tag to identify its owner and protector, but Christ gives us His royal robes of righteousness and the protection and power of the Holy Spirit.

Listen to the voice of Jesus gently calling you by name. He invites you to enter His Kingdom … to sit at His table … to journey with Him now and throughout the ages.

To draw you to Himself, the Lord uses love, not shame, and encouragement, not blame. As you draw near to God, you'll learn to accept His unconditional love and your position in heavenly places. Jesus proved His love on the cross when He bought your freedom.

The story doesn't end there. Jesus has more gifts He wants to give you.

Are you eager to receive them? The Apostle Paul was sure eager to share the good news about God's gifts as he wrote a letter to the early church to encourage them to make their hearts ready to receive such gifts. Listen to his prayer and prepare your own heart to be open, and ready to receive and enjoy all of the other promised gifts:

> I pray that the eyes of your heart may be enlightened in order that you may know the hope to which he has called you, the riches of his glorious inheritance in his holy people, and his incomparably great power for us who believe.[8]

---

[8] Ephesians 1:18–19.

The next chapter reveals the gift of new names and positions for those who believe. It's followed by chapters outlining the gift of precious promises of the incomparable great power of Christ, plus how to receive this glorious inheritance simply by receiving the ultimate gift of Jesus Himself.

Letter to God: Acknowledging the Gift of You

Oh, how I marvel at all of your creation. I stand in awe of the way you orchestrated the universe to provide meaning through the circle of life.

How special and precious is the creation of life. How amazing that it's designed within a set of perfect gifts — beginning with us as a present to Jesus.

It's your gifts that provide meaning, fulfillment, and joy. It's where the true journey begins, a place deep within our hearts, and at the depths of our souls.

To all who would ask, to all who seek, we open our minds to the mysteries so deep.

What joy you, too, feel when you make yourself known through the giving of gifts.

You gave us to Jesus, your one and only Son, to be the guardian of the gift of our life — for He is the gateway of heaven, the doorway to our soul. Through Him you reveal to our world, within each man's heart, the meaning and mystery of each man's life.

What was long hidden has now been exposed —
but only to those who will give glory to the one
He has told.

So, I long for the gifts that you would bestow, to
learn more about you, and to love you untold.

I choose to receive the Gift of You.

So, please open my eyes, my ears, and my
heart. I want to know and embrace each gift
you bestow. I want to be made complete as I
embrace, behold, and treasure you more highly
than man seeks out gold.

I will pursue you in every corner of my world.
I will embrace each moment of time spent
with you.

The journey is before me, and I answer the call.
I will live for you, through you, and with you,
every moment of my life.

Love, your forever child.

Chapter 3
Gift of New Names

As she played with her new puppy, Jenny asked her mother, "What shall I name her?"

"Honey, that's up to you," her mom replied. "I know you'll pick out just the right name."

"She does have a white tip on one paw, so maybe 'Tippy'? But, she also has a lot of black, so maybe 'Shadow'? Hmmm, this is hard. I want just the right name."

Jenny had fun picking out a name for her puppy. As Jenny lay on the floor next to her puppy, she whispered, "Rachel...Ribbon?" Just then, to get Jenny's attention, the puppy jumped, grabbed Jenny's hair, and began tugging. "Oh, you rascal... hmmm ... 'Rascal'? No, that doesn't really fit. But, maybe it will make a good nickname if you keep this up!"

Jenny tried peering into the future as she contemplated various names. What kind of dog would her puppy become? As she read through hundreds of names listed on the Internet, she contemplated "Zoey," which means "life"; "Lexi," which stands for "defender"; and "Anna," which means "gracious." They all sounded so good, but none of them felt just right.

After a few days and dozens of attempts, Jenny asked her mom what she thought of "Bessie."

"That's a lovely name. Why is it special to you?"

"Well, I've always been wanting a little sister," Jenny mused, "but it also had to be a name that fit a dog. 'Bessie' was the name of that cute calf at the farm, and 'Bessie' was also the name of the farmer's herding dog that protected the farm animals ... oh, I can't explain it, Mom. It just feels right."

"Then that's the name you should give her," Jenny's mom responded, and then added, "Did

you know the name 'Bessie' is a Hebrew baby name that comes from Elisheba, which has the meaning of 'God is satisfaction'?"

"Oh, then it's perfect!" chirped Jenny. "Bessie is a gift from God, and we are both satisfied!"

Names for pets matter. For humans, names matter, too. One of the hardest decisions parents make is picking out a name to put on the birth certificate. Just Google "book of baby names" or "list of baby names," and you'll be overwhelmed with three hundred million web pages offering suggestions.

Jesus' Name

Names are also a big deal for Jesus. We know that He went by many names that reflected His character. A few of the more common ones are: *Christ, Good Shepherd, Immanuel, King of Kings, Lamb of God, Master, Messiah, Redeemer, and Savior.*

There are dozens of other names you may not know. I've listed some of them for you on the next page and a full list in the Appendix at the back of this book. Jesus wants you to call Him by one of His names when you talk to Him, just like you want to be greeted by your name by your friends.

These other names help you know Jesus more personally. In fact, each of these names represents an attribute or characteristic of Christ. It gives you insight into how marvelous Jesus really is. Contemplate the majesty of Christ Jesus as you read this longer list of His names:

Advocate	*Friend*	*Prince of Peace*
Alpha	*Fountain*	*Rock*
and Omega	*Gate*	*Ruler*
Bread of Life	*High Priest*	*Sure Foundation*
Cornerstone	*Light of*	*Teacher*
Deliverer	*the World*	*The Beginning*
Faithful	*Mediator*	*The Way*
and True	*One and Only*	*Wonderful*
Foundation		*Counselor*

Names are equally important to God the Father, and He goes by dozens of names, too, because they also help describe Him and His perfect character. Here are just a few of God the Father's names:

Abba Father	*King of Heaven*
Ancient of Days	*Righteous Father*
God Almighty	*The God of All Comfort*
God of Abraham, Isaac,	*The Great and Awesome*
and Jacob	*God*

It's no wonder why people, the children of God, care so much about names. The names of humans aren't just important to us — they are also very significant to God. Throughout the Bible, God was in the business of giving humans new names. Sometimes, He changed a person's name when He planned a special task for them.

Abraham's Name

Consider Abram and Sarai. You probably know them better as Abraham and Sarah.[9] When God entered into an eternal covenant with Abram, He changed their names.

In his native language, the name "Abram" literally meant "Exalted Father." That's a powerful name. However, at the age of ninety-nine, Abram still had no children. Can you imagine what he had to go through almost daily when someone greeted Abram and asked him his name? It might have gone something like this:

A visitor approached Abram and said, "Hello, my name is Wanderer of the Land, I have traveled many countries. I am pleased to say that I find your village very pleasing. It flows with milk and honey. I am hoping you will grant me passage through your land. May I ask by what name do you go by so that I can greet you properly?"

"Greetings, brother, Wanderer of the Land. I am known as Exalted Father, and I am pleased to offer you comfort and a warm meal as you continue on your journey."

"Thank you, Exalted Father. I would be honored to stay with you. By the way, Exalted Father, how many sons do you have?"

"I have no sons."

The Wanderer was unable to hide his look of surprise, but he quipped, "Ah, yes, 'Exalted Father' — then how many daughters do you have?"

---

[9] Genesis 17:5, 15.

"I have no daughters."

With stunned silence, Wanderer was lost for words. But, he managed to muster a kind reply, before quickly changing the subject. "At least you seem to be in good health ... how is the weather in this lovely valley?"

It must have been like salt on an open wound whenever Abram welcomed a new guest into his home or even interacted with his friends. Perhaps he hid in his tent sometimes to keep from reliving the pain of each new encounter or the morning greeting.

I think that if I were Abram, I might have said: "If I hear just one more time, 'Good morning, Exalted Father, I wish you a prosperous day' ... I am going to scream. I'll 'prosper' you over the head with my staff if you don't stop calling me 'Exalted Father'!"

One day God met with Abram. (As amazing as it sounds, Abram got visits from God Himself.) In that brief encounter, God announced that He planned to give Abram a new name. It must have been a welcome relief. No more teasing by the neighbors or shocked looks on faces of new acquaintances.

The moment of anticipation was upon him. Perhaps Abram hoped God would give him a new name such as "Chosen One" or "Faithful Servant." It might have played out like this:

"Abram?" God called.

"Yes, my God, I am here."

"Abram, you have found favor in my eyes because you are faithful. I have heard your cries and moans. I have come to comfort you. I will bless you."

"My God, I am unworthy of your great love and blessings."

"Abram, I have many promises to give to you. I also have a new name for you."

"My God, I am your servant — may your will be done."

His anticipation must have matched Jenny's on Christmas day. Abram's mind might have raced as he thought, "A new name! A name selected by God Himself! God has heard my cries. He has seen my affliction. Now my family and friends will look upon me with respect."

"Abram, you will no longer be called 'Exalted Father,' but now you will be known to the entire world as *Abraham*. You will be called *'Father of Many.'*"

I don't know about Abraham, but I would have been stunned. Talk about disappointment. Honestly, I would have been hurt or even angry.

I may have tried reasoning with God. "Thank you, Father God. Well, uhm … it's not that I am ungrateful, but can we either keep this name just between us, or perhaps you can give me a nickname to share with others. I mean, well, it was pretty darn hard telling people my name when it was 'Exalted Father,' but 'Father of Many' — well, that is going to make it even worse."

But, that is not how Abraham responded. He was thrilled over his new name. Abraham knew the God of many names so well that he believed God at His word. God was saying that, by some miracle — even at the age of one hundred — he would father many children.

At this point in time, however, God didn't snap His finger and instantly make Abraham's wife pregnant. All Abraham was given was a promise that, one day in the future, this old, barren couple, though good as dead, would be the ancestors of many nations.

Can you imagine what transpired after Abraham left the tent and told his tribe that he actually met with God and that God spoke to him? Even though it had happened many times, I am sure they always asked him to prove that he had met with God. The people likely questioned Abram, "What sign can you offer us that this is true?"

"I have no miraculous sign, but God changed my name!"

This silenced the crowd. They thought, *Yes, that would be a merciful act of God to see Abram's plight and rescue him from this misery. That would be what we think God would do.*

"What mighty name did he give to you, Abram, Exalted Father and honored leader of our tribe?"

"My new name is…"

With anticipation, the people waited to hear the new, majestic name given to someone so favored that God would audibly speak to them.

"God named me *Abraham!*"

You can almost hear the snickering. They all knew the name meant *Father of Many*. They must have thought God was joking or, worse yet, that "Abraham" was senile.

Many must have thought, "No, Abram did not meet with God. There is no way God would make a joke of him like that."

I would have been one of the ones shaking my head in disbelief. I would have viewed Abraham (or would I still be tempted to call him "Abram"?) as a childless, hopeless man of ninety-nine, and doubted God's promise of granting him children.

Abraham was not like others. He boasted in his new name. He believed God. He kept his head high as he proclaimed that God sealed the promise with this name, and that one day he would have so many children that they'll be as grains of sand on the beach, and that leaders of nations will arise from his line.

While it seemed impossible at the time, Abraham believed his new name and became known as the Father of our Faith.

Sometime later, past the age of one hundred, God indeed fulfilled this promise, giving Abraham several children and many grandchildren. Today, his offspring outnumber the grains of sand on a beach.

Can you imagine the look on the faces of all those that had doubted his sanity since the day he claimed to have met with God? He was one hundred years old. That is a century. Today, if anyone lives that long, the President of the United States sends them a congratulatory letter.

Abraham got his new name and children to boot. In fact, Abraham is today known as a Father of Many Nations.[10] He also remains a father figure to us, since the human lineage to the child Christ went through Abraham. God chose this name on purpose to signify Abraham's purpose.

Sarah's Name

The story of his wife, Sarah, is equally as fascinating. Her original name, *Sarai* means "dominating." It was actually consistent with her character. She was the wife of the boss. What she said had to be done. On at least one occasion, we know that Sarah was harsh when treating one of her maidservants. In fact, she banished the servant and her son (who had been fathered by Abraham!) into the desert, knowing that it was essentially a death sentence.[11]

Sarai must have had a real dominating personality for Abraham to agree with her exile of his firstborn son. Sarai had also been responsible for the birth of the boy. She had offered her maidservant to Abraham to move things along, after several years had passed and Sarai had had no children, despite God's promise of making Abraham a father. She had dominated things then and

---

[10] Romans 4:17.
[11] Genesis 21.

did so again when she decided she had had enough of the maidservant and her son.

Yet, God, in His mercy, gave Sarai a new name, too. She would be called "Sarah," which means *princess*. God also changed her heart so that she grew into her new title, as Abraham grew into his. Sarah is now listed in the New Testament as one among "the great cloud of witnesses" who lived by faith.[12] God also gave her children, as promised.

Biblical Names

Knowing the importance of names, Abraham and Sarah carefully chose their first son's name. "Isaac" means *laughter*. It may be a twist upon the laughter they felt when told at an elderly age that they would have children, as well as the pure joy over the promise fulfilled at his birth!

Jacob, the son of Isaac, is another example of a new name given by God. While growing up, Jacob made an enemy of his older brother, Esau. First, he convinced Esau to trade his inheritance rights of a firstborn for a bowl of stew.[13] Second, by dressing in Esau's clothes, Jacob tricked his father into granting him, as the younger son, the royal blessings of the firstborn.[14]

A brother can only take so much trickery. Esau was much stronger and more powerful in the tribe. He set his heart upon revenge and plotted to kill Jacob. This

---

[12] Hebrews 12:1, 11–12.
[13] Genesis 25:31–33.
[14] Genesis 27:1–36.

left Jacob with little option but to flee to a distant land. That's where God shaped his character.

In the fullness of time, Jacob was called by God to return to his homeland. As he got near his hometown, Jacob became overwhelmed with fear. The night before Jacob's fateful reunion with Esau, someone snuck into camp. God had taken human form and physically wrestled Jacob. By all accounts, it was a fight to the death. Jacob could not break free from the grip of what he thought was a bandit out to rob and kill him.

Exhausted but hanging on, Jacob finally realized it was God.[15] For the first time, he had a desperate heart to know God intimately. Now, Jacob held a tight grip on the God-man, and said he would not let go until God would grant him a blessing and become a guidepost for his life. The Lord was pleased to grant the request.

After changing Jacob's deceitful and independent heart, God changed Jacob's name to "Israel," which means *Wrestles with God.*[16]

Jacob came to realize that God used the wrestling match to show how, like so many of us, he had fought his entire life against God, instead of submitting to the Lord's will.

After that night, the life of Jacob was forever changed. He became a needy, obedient servant and friend of the Living Lord.

---

[15] Genesis 32:22–31.
[16] Genesis 32:27–28.

In the New Testament, God changed more of His followers' names. He changed Simon to "Peter," which means *Rock*.[17] In fact, he went from Simon-the-hard-of-hearing to Peter-the-firm-in-faith.

Although it's not clear if God directly changed Saul's name, we do know that, after his conversion, Saul went by "Paul."[18] Saul changed from a wanton persecutor of Christians to a willing prisoner of Christ.

What's Your Name?

How about you? What name(s) do you go by? Perhaps you've taken on a few aliases. If you use e-mail, Facebook, Twitter, or other social media, you may have several screen names. One thing about using a name is that you often end up modeling your behavior after its meaning. It was true for Biblical characters, and it is likely true for you.

Here's the good news. God changed your name the day you became a gift to Jesus. That's right. God is giving you some new names...family names, the names reserved for His children.

Just as Jenny named her puppy, Jesus has named you. Here are some pet names Jesus has for you:

> *Adopted Son/Daughter of God, Ambassador of Christ, Brother to Jesus, Child of God, Chosen by God, Citizen of Heaven, Dearly Loved, Friend*

---

[17] John 1:42.
[18] Acts 9:1–19, 22:6–21.

> *of Jesus, Future Judge of Angels, God's Heir,*
> *God's Holy People, God's Possession, God's*
> *Workmanship, Image of God, Member of God's*
> *Household, New Creation, Righteousness of*
> *God, Royal Priest, Saint, Salt and Light of the*
> *World, Temple of the Holy Spirit, Wonderfully*
> *Created.*[19]

Wow. Those are a lot of new names. Not only that, but they have some incredible characteristics and meanings. As if that were not enough, these are the names given to you by God Himself!

Because these are your new names, you'll need to take them on and become familiar with them. Why not practice right now? Read the names below with proper prefatory phrases in front of each one to drive home the point. As you do, ask God to open your heart to Him.

> God calls me an *Adopted Son/Daughter of God.*
> God calls me an *Ambassador of Christ.*
> God calls me a *Brother/Sister to Jesus.*
> God calls me a *Child of God.*
> God calls me *Chosen by God.*
> God calls me a *Citizen of Heaven.*
> God calls me *Dearly Loved.*
> God calls me a *Friend of Jesus.*

---

[19] The biblical references to these names are in the Appendix.

God calls me a *Future Judge of Angels*.
God calls me His *Heir*.
God calls me His *Holy People*.
God calls me His *Possession*.
God calls me His *Workmanship*.
God calls me made in the *Image of God*.
God calls me a *Member of His Household*.
God calls me a *New Creation*.
God calls me the *Righteousness of God*.
God calls me a *Royal Priest*.
God calls me a *Saint*.
God calls me *Salt and Light of the World*.
God calls me a *Temple of the Holy Spirit*.
God calls me *Wonderfully Created*.

It's okay if you feel overwhelmed, but don't shrink back. These new names are truly yours, even if they may take some time and energy to fully grow into them.

You may need to wrestle with God, like Jacob did, before you fully surrender, but the names still hold true. God sees into your heart and soul, and He knows your future.

Maybe you have been a bit like Sarai, pushy or demanding. But, you can now choose to start acting like Sarah, a princess of the Lord Jesus Christ. You can also stop being merely a hearer of the word like Simon and become a doer like Peter. You can stop thinking egotistically like Saul and start becoming a patron like Paul.

Just like Abraham, who proudly wore the new name of Father of Many well before having a child, you can start wearing these new names now, before you're fully refined. As you decide to go by the names Jesus has already given you, you'll start purposefully living out these characteristics and becoming the obedient, grateful, thankful, content son or daughter of Jesus you were destined to become.

Mark this page and return here whenever you doubt God's love for you or when you want to be strengthened in faith. These are your new names — names you're destined to grow into just like everyone else to whom God has given a new name!

As you keep striving to faithfully wear your new names, know this: Jesus is eagerly waiting to give you one more final name on the day you enter heaven and reign with Him for all eternity. It is a name that not only is unique to you but a new name that has never even been whispered by anyone before. The Bible describes this about the new heavenly name Jesus has waiting for you:

> *I will give you a white stone with a new name written on it, known only to the one who receives it.*[20]

The story doesn't end here. Jesus, the gift giver, has more special gifts and promises He wants to give you.

---

[20] Revelation 2:17.

Modern-Day Psalm: Name above all names.

Glory be to the one and only true living Son of God and Father; the one whose name is above all names.

May praise be forevermore to the Lamb of God, Jesus Christ our Lord!

Who can count the glorious deeds He has performed?
Who can grasp the infinite love He pours forth?
He alone deserves worship and adoration!

The One who created the world has authority to judge His creation.
Yet, mercy and grace pour out from Him.
His patience and long-suffering have no end!

Oh that we should be called Children of God.
Oh that we are invited to live eternally in His presence.
Oh what precious gifts He bestows—gifts beyond what can be imagined, earned, or bargained for.

With awe and a joyful spirit, I shall forever praise the Son of God whose name is above all names.

Chapter 4

Gift of Precious Promises

"Sit, no, no, sit, sit, good girl, Bessie, sit, yes sit. Oh, good girl, Bessie! Good, sit, good, sit."

JENNY'S PUPPY WASN'T born housetrained or knowing all the commands that pleased her owner. Jenny needed to spend a lot of time training and encouraging her precious puppy.

Jesus knows that you are human. He knows you need training. He knows your life works better when you obey His commands.

Jesus wants you to succeed. He also wants you to keep growing closer to Him and even become more like Him. Jesus knows you can't do these things on your own. Therefore, He is right there with you, giving you His divine power and making promises you can count on. Try this promise on for size:

> His divine power has given to us all things that pertain to life and godliness, through the knowledge of Him who called us by glory and virtue, as His divine power has given to us all things that pertain to life and godliness, through the knowledge of Him who called us by glory and virtue, by which have been given to us exceedingly great and precious promises, that through these you may be partakers of the divine nature...[21]

Because you are a child of God, with the names of God, you're entitled to each one of the many precious promises of God. Next are just a handful of the hundreds of promises, pledges, and assurances that Jesus makes to you.

Here are some of the promises of Jesus.

Renew your strength and give you courage

> Even youths grow tired and weary, and young men stumble and fall; but those who hope in the Lord will renew their strength.

---

[21] 2 Peter 1:3–4.

They will soar on wings like eagles; they will run and not grow weary, will walk and not be faint.[22]

So do not fear, for I am with you; do not be dismayed, for I am your God. I will strengthen you and help you; I will uphold you with my righteous right hand.[23]

Be strong and courageous. Do not be afraid or terrified because of them, for the Lord your God goes with you; he will never leave you or forsake you.[24]

Grant you prosperity and hope

For I know the plans I have for you, declares the Lord, plans to prosper you and not to harm you, plans to give you hope and a future.[25]

Replace fear and anxiety with peace

Do not be anxious about anything, but in every situation, by prayer and petition, with

[22] Isaiah 40:30–31.
[23] Isaiah 41:10.
[24] Deuteronomy 31:6.
[25] Jeremiah 29:11.

thanksgiving, present your requests to God. And the peace of God, which transcends all understanding, will guard your hearts and your minds in Christ Jesus.[26]

Forgive all your sins

If we confess our sins, he is faithful and just and will forgive us our sins and purify us from all unrighteousness.[27]

Love you forever

For I am convinced that neither death nor life, neither angels nor demons, neither the present nor the future, nor any powers, neither height nor depth, nor anything else in all creation, will be able to separate us from the love of God that is in Christ Jesus our Lord.[28]

Do not fear, for I have redeemed you; I have summoned you by name; you are mine.[29]

---

[26] Philippians 4:6–7.
[27] 1 John 1:9.
[28] Romans 8:38–39.
[29] Isaiah 43:1.

Comfort you

Even though I walk through the darkest valley, I will fear no evil, for you are with me; your rod and your staff, they comfort me.[30]

Praise be to the God and Father of our Lord Jesus Christ, the Father of compassion and the God of all comfort, who comforts us in all our troubles, so that we can comfort those in any trouble with the comfort we ourselves receive from God.[31]

Give you rest

Come to me, all you who are weary and burdened, and I will give you rest. Take my yoke upon you and learn from me, for I am gentle and humble in heart, and you will find rest for your souls.[32]

Give you wisdom

If any of you lacks wisdom, you should ask God, who gives generously to all without finding fault, and it will be given to you.[33]

---

[30] Psalm 23:4.
[31] 2 Corinthians 1:3–4.
[32] Matthew 11:28–29.
[33] James 1:5.

Provide a way of escape from temptation

> No temptation has overtaken you except what is common to mankind. And God is faithful; he will not let you be tempted beyond what you can bear. But when you are tempted, he will also provide a way out so that you can endure it.[34]

Fulfill the desires of your heart

> Take delight in the Lord, and he will give you the desires of your heart.[35]

Okay, catch your breath. Each one of these promises is yours. Cling to them.

Although all of His promises are too numerous to list here, the simple message is that the Lord is in the business of restoration, not condemnation — building up, not tearing down. He is your "refuge and strength, an ever-present help in trouble."[36]

As if you're not overwhelmed enough, allow me to add just a few of my favorite promises. These are two lesser-known, but striking promises that may blow you away. I call these two my *"wow!"* verses:

---

[34] 1 Corinthians 10:13.
[35] Psalm 37:4.
[36] Psalm 46:1.

The Lord **confides** in those who fear him;
he makes his covenant known to them.[37]

The **secret** things belong to the Lord our
God, but the things revealed belong to us
and to our children forever, that we may
follow all the words of this law.[38]

The God who formed you from dust and created the
entire universe by simply speaking it into existence tells
you that He desires to *confide* in you and to share with
you *secret things that only belong to God.*
Wow!
That was the only word I could actually muster when
I first read these verses.
Wow! Maybe God really does love me.
Wow! Maybe Jesus really does consider me family!
Of course, with every relationship, there is an obli-
gation. As children of God entrusted with the mysteries
of God, we have been given a trust. We are required to
prove faithful by obeying Christ.[39] It's our calling and
our new nature.
Here is how it works. When you're awed by God,
it naturally leads you to go all in for Jesus...to give up
control...and to center your entire life around Him.

---

[37] Psalm 25:14.
[38] Deuteronomy 29:29.
[39] 1 Corinthians 4:1–2.

The more you yield and draw near to God, the more He draws near to you. Then, the more your Master trusts you and reveals to you the many mighty wonders that are hidden from the rest of the world. Jesus will continually reveal more and more wonders to you as you keep yielding to Him — so much so that you'll remain captivated for life!

That's why I want to fall on my face — just like Peter fell at Jesus' knees in fearful recognition that He was Lord of the Universe and muttered, "Go away from me, Lord; I am a sinful man!"[40]

Peter had spent all night fishing with his large nets in the bay, but had caught nothing. Not a single minnow. He and his crew were tired. They pulled into shore and were just about to drag the heavy nets onto shore to clean, mend, and store them before they could finally go to bed.

But, a crowd of early risers had already discovered that Jesus was at the shore. They pressed in so tightly that Jesus asked Peter if he could put the boat out a short distance so Jesus could use Peter's boat as a platform to preach to the crowds.

Perhaps grudgingly, Peter agreed. Perhaps a bit curiously, too. He had heard so much about this man who purportedly performed miracles. "Okay," Peter said as he pushed the boat back from the shore.

---

[40] Luke 5:8.

Jesus got in the boat.

A short sermon may have begun fine, but this guy kept talking. One story after another he shared to a growing crowd. Peter started to get restless. We've all been there. On a Sunday morning when we have places to be, we secretly start hoping that the preacher would just land the plane already.

Curious or not, Peter was dead tired. I suspect that, even in the presence of the greatest preacher of all times, Peter must've had a hard time keeping his eyes open, out of sheer exhaustion. He may have been just a little anxious to pull into shore because he was now further behind schedule and still had hard work to do.

Then an unthinkable happened. After Jesus dismissed the crowd and jumped off the boat, He didn't thank Peter and send him to bed. Rather, Jesus told Peter, "Put out into deep water and let down the nets for a catch."

Peter's mind must have raced. "Really? He knew that we fished all night and caught nothing. First, He borrows our boat so that we can't clean the nets. Now He tells us how to fish? It's backbreaking work to let the nets down and pull them back in. Really? For what? What does this carpenter know about fishing?"

You can almost hear the sarcasm in Peter's response, "Master, we've worked hard all night and haven't caught anything. But, *because you say so*, I will let down the nets."

I imagine that the "because you say so" was dripping with insincerity. Perhaps it was because there were still some in the crowd there who believed Jesus really was the Messiah that Peter felt obligated to do as He requested, even though it would be a total waste of time.

Peter obliged. He moved the boat out just far enough to make it look good. He even let down *one* of his nets. Peter likely was simply going through the motions to get it over with. Perhaps, in the back of his mind, he had a hint of pride so that, after they pulled up another round of empty nets, he could say, "I told you so" to this guy everyone was mesmerized by.

What happened next is amazing. His net was immediately filled with such a large number of fish that it began to break. He needed the help of another boat. They filled not one boat, but two boats with fish. More fish than ever...more fish than humanly possible. The boats were so full that they began to sink.

That's when the old Simon got it. That's when the new Peter fell on his knees in total awe. That's when, in real repentance, he proclaimed his unbelief and sinful nature, and finally desired to go all in for Christ. That was Peter's first *Wow!* moment.

That's the *Wow!* I felt reading those two passages about how God wanted to confide in me and share His secrets with me. I wanted to cry out, "Go away from me, Lord; I am a sinful man!"

The good news is that, yes, I am a sinful man, but, no, Jesus will never drive me (or you) away. He promises just the opposite. We already know that He promises to *renew, forgive, prosper, strengthen, love, cherish, and comfort.*

The *Wow!* moment is like the spark needed to start a fire. However, as humans, we need to figure out how to take the next steps.

The first step seemed fairly straightforward to Peter: he immediately left his boats to follow Jesus. But, the next steps in the journey were a lot less clear to him. He had no formal training, no roadmap, and no clue what tomorrow looked like.

Even though Peter walked with Jesus for three years, at times he and the other disciples asked the same basic questions as we all do: "How do I pray?"[41] or "How many times must I forgive others?"[42]

Some of us have a hard time believing that God will keep His promises. At times, we all struggle to hear His voice or even know what direction to go. That's all part of the journey. The key is to spend time with Jesus and to keep our eyes and heart open.

The Psalm 119 Challenge

One of the things that helped me start taking the next steps is what I call the "Psalm 119 Challenge." Set aside about ten minutes this week to read Psalm 119:1–40, and pick out five verses that have the greatest impact on you.

---

[41] Luke 11:1.
[42] Matthew 18:21–22.

When someone gave me this challenge a dozen years ago, I thought it would be too easy at first.

"Really, pick five verses out of forty? How hard can that be?"

What happened next was amazing. As I read through the forty verses once, many passages jumped out at me. That's when I began to take the challenge more seriously. It was much harder than I thought. There were about a dozen verses that hit me hard and left my heart and soul standing on edge.

Over the next fifteen minutes, I tried again and again to whittle down my favorites to five, as I read and reread the forty verses. What happened was that I fell in love with all of Psalm 119 that day. (And, I am still not sure I can limit myself to five favorite verses!)

In fact, this challenge created in me a love for *all* of the Psalms. Up until that time, I had basically limited myself to reading the New Testament. After falling in love with Psalm 119, I craved the Psalms. What's more, I began writing my own Psalms, even though I had always felt like I didn't even have a poetic right brain.

My Bible was soon filled with underlining and highlighting throughout the entire book of Psalms, with hundreds of "favorite" verses.

Next, I took on Proverbs with my yellow highlighter and blue ink pen. I kept circling words and making notes in the margins. I began asking God to reveal Himself in the words. I had developed a deep desire to know God by knowing His Word.

New favorite verses and more precious promises of God were finding their way to my joyfully growing list!

The experience so filled me with inspiration that, afterwards, I went back to the New Testament and started at the beginning, circling and marking up my new favorite verses and promises in every book. Today, I cannot read a Bible without a pen in my hand. I also have note pads filled with my thoughts and impressions from reading the Bible. The end result is that, for almost every situation that comes up in my life or the life of a friend, I have a circled verse that guides me.

I can't promise you that you will absolutely fall in love with Scripture and Jesus the Author if you take the Psalm 119 challenge, as I did. But, I encourage you to open your heart to that possibility!

What I can attest is that the best way to know and receive God's precious promises is to spend time with God as you read the very words He has written to and for you.

Modern-Day Psalm: Promises

In you, I am made strong. I will not be afraid, for you are always with me.
I will soar like wings of eagles. I will roar like the mighty lion.

In your strong arms, I find rest. Knowing your goodness softens my heart and fills my soul.

No longer will I be guided by my own plans or trust in riches that fade.

I open my heart and trust in you alone.

I will not be anxious or afraid because I can see your face.

My soul is comforted when I speak of my innermost thoughts, hopes, and dreams. I am at peace because I know you hear me and are always near.

I rest in knowing that there is no power on earth or in the skies above that can make you break a promise.

Your loving kindness delivers freedom and
sustains me.

I rest secure in your love — a love that has no
bounds.

How precious are your promises! I rest in them
each day.

Flood me with your love.

Make known to me your plans, for I take
delight in you, my Lord, Master, and King.

Chapter 5

Gift of Jesus

JESUS WANTS TO GIVE YOU presents because He loves you more than anything in the universe. In fact, Jesus picked out the perfect gift for you before you were even born. It was something priceless and something only He could give, more precious than silver or gold — a gift that would cost Jesus everything.

God's Creation

Genesis, the first book of the Bible, is God's story to us about how He made the universe — including the stars, the earth, and every living creature — all in anticipation of and creation for man. The Bible tells us that the whole earth and universe were made by God for man.

On the first day, God made matter and light.

On the second day, God created a divide between heaven and earth, and began preparing the place for man to dwell.

On the third day, God divided the land from the sea and created vegetation.

On the fourth day, God created the sun, moon, and the vast array of stars in the sky.

On the fifth day, God created all the living animals.

With everything perfectly in place, the world was ready for man to live in as the guardian of the rest of creation.

On the sixth and final day,[43] God created man.

At that moment, God also gave mankind the entire world as a gift. The first gift God gave to humans was the entire world. Here's what God said to Adam and Eve:

> Grow in number. Fill the earth and rule over it. Rule over the fish of the sea, over the birds of the sky, and over every living thing that moves on the earth. Then God said, See, I have given you every plant that gives seeds that is on the earth, and every tree that has fruit that gives seeds. They will be food for you. I have given every green plant for food to every animal of the earth,

---

[43] The next day, God said He was done with creation of the universe and called the day "Sabbath," meaning a day of rest and an example that people should have a day of rest once a week as a rhythm of life. Genesis 2:2–3; see also Hebrews 4:1–11.

and to every bird of the sky, and to every
thing that moves on the earth that has life.

Wow! God gave man the authority to rule over the
entire world! That's some special gift.

As wonderful and awesome as the gift of earth was,
it was not the most precious gift that Jesus intended
for man. We don't spend much time thinking back on
the exact moment when God made man, but hidden
in one small passage is the story of the immeasurable
love God had for you, a gift so amazing that it even
tops the earth!

At the start of day six, this is what happened, as
recorded in Genesis:

> Then God said, 'Let us make man like us
> and let him be head over the fish of the sea,
> and over the birds of the air, and over the
> cattle, and over all the earth, and over every
> thing that moves on the ground.'[44]

God recorded His own conversation for us about
how He decided to create the world and man. In this
record, He is sharing with you His innermost thinking
and secrets.

There are six words that really jump out. God said,
"'Let **us** make man like **us**!'"

---

[44] Genesis 1:26–27.

This passage helps us understand who God really is and how we fit into the universe. It begins by focusing on who God was referring to when He said "us."

The Trinity

Although it's beyond our full comprehension, it's clear that God was speaking of Himself. That's how we first know that, although God is One, He exists in three persons: God the Father, God the Son, and God the Holy Spirit. This is why Christians refer to God as "The Trinity."

Each of the three personhoods of God is unique, yet intertwined and inseparable from the other and consists of just One God. Each personhood has different identities and roles, but yet fulfill the same purpose and actually form part of the same Godhead and all three of which are equally and fully and eternally God. All three are necessary, all three are distinct, and yet all three are One.

As a child, I once tried to understand The Trinity as a piece of rope with three separate strands of string wrapped together. But, that didn't come close to explaining God. Nothing we can look to can explain God. He, meaning all three persons, had no beginning. Although they each have their own personality, they cannot live or function independently. Yet, all three in One have unlimited power, unlimited knowledge, unlimited everything. Don't forget, with just words, God spoke the world — the entire universe — into existence!

If you say, "Well, it doesn't make sense to me," then I am glad. As humans, we can't fully understand or explain God. Of course, none of us can fully understand or explain electricity, either. Even Einstein admitted he didn't understand electricity, but went on to use and rely on it.

Let's leave aside the profound mystery of The Trinity for a moment. Let's return to the day that God had a conversation with Himself regarding creating man.

Allow me some creative storytelling to make the point.

As I imagine it, God the Father addressed the Son and Spirit and asked, "What if we were to create man in our image?"

Both the Son and Spirit, in unison, replied, "Yes, Father, it would be grand!"

In the twinkling of an eye, all three envisioned the same thought. In human terms, the entire lifetime of mankind flashed before their eyes. They instantly saw every minute detail of every human's life from day one through the end of human time. They foresaw every joy, every pain, every hurt, and every gain. Nothing escaped them. They knew the life of every president, king, and criminal. They knew the day of each birth and death of every creature, and every moment in between. They even knew the number of hairs on everyone's head. They wiped every tear and received every praise beforehand.

They even saw and knew that, by giving man a free will to make choices, many people would deny that God even existed. God also saw that men would engage in wars over land. Some would even make other nations slaves. There would be bloodshed, hate, and evil in the land.

But, God the Father spoke about seeing the good — the light shining from the dark, the hope, and the victories against all odds. In the struggle, there would be great joy. Good would triumph over evil.

The Spirit spoke next, "Yes, Father, I agree. I also know what it requires. I would dwell among men. I would gently lead and guide them as their conscience, whispering what is right, true, and noble."

God the Father smiled. "Yes, Spirit, it means all of that. It also means you will grieve when men do not listen. It will cut deeply. It will hurt more than even the world can bear."

"Yes, Father, I know. I see what you see. We both see the struggles and the pains, yet we both know that it is still good and worthy."

Before Jesus spoke, with almost-sorrowful eyes, God the Father turned to the Son and said, "My Son, my one and only Begotten Son. You also see what must be done. But, we will, indeed, make man in our image only if you agree."

"Yes, Father, I see what you see. I know what must be done. But, it is my great privilege and joy. I know that, in the fullness of time, when their sins are great, I must leave our heavenly abode to dwell with man in the form of a man. I know there is no other way. I know that one innocent must take the punishment of the guilty. I also know that many will deny me, deny you, and remain ignorant of the Spirit. I know that they will crucify me. But, I also know that there is no other way. We cannot create man unless I am ready to do this."

"Yes, Son. It means all of that. It also means I must cast all of the punishment of every sin of man onto you. For that moment, I must actually look away from you as you become sin. It will grieve me more than anything to do that. But, you will rise from the dead and take your place back here by my side. You will be given a name above all names so that, at even the mention of your name — "Jesus" — every knee in heaven and on earth in the fullness of time will bow and acknowledge that you are one with God, my Son."

Then, with great joy, all three agreed as One, and it is recorded:

> And God made man in His own likeness. In
> the likeness of God He made him.[45]

There you have it. God made you and me (and every human being) in His very own likeness.

This Bible passage and, indeed, this revelation by God about our creation is so powerful that it formed the very basis for the foundation of our great nation, and is the underpinning of the Declaration of Independence

[45] Genesis 1:27.

that established the United States of America on July 4, 1776, and was the guidepost of our young nation for twelve years before the Constitution was adopted. Here are the famous words of the Declaration of Independence:

> We hold these truths to be self-evident, that all men are created equal, that they are endowed by their Creator with certain unalienable Rights, that among these are Life, Liberty, and the pursuit of Happiness.

Yes, it's self-evident that all human life is precious to God, and that He grants us rights that cannot be taken away.

In the image of our Triune God, we were also given body, mind, and spirit. Each part of our bodies is amazing, whether we take notice of our ever-present heartbeat, or breathe, or count the steps taken by our feet each day. God also gave us inquisitive minds that can ponder and explore the vast array of stars and deep blue oceans. He gave us a spirit-filled drive and determination to go along with our emotions and free will. Yes, how fearfully and wonderfully we have been created in the image of God.

As incredible as this gift of life and likeliness is, we were never meant to walk alone. Because we remain incomplete unless we journey with our Creator, God also gave us an innate need to seek and find Jesus — the only place of true happiness and satisfaction. That's why the question of the ages has always been, "How do I find and enjoy Jesus?"

The Predicament

The simple gift and message of the Gospel of Jesus gets a lot less complicated when we pare it down to the bare essentials. It begins prior to the creation of the world. It begins with Heaven, where our Triune God dwells. Heaven is such a perfect place that no sin can enter it.[46]

The day that God determined to make man was the same day that heaven and earth, as we know them, became separate. Beginning on Day One, there would be Heaven, where God in all His glory would remain, and there would be earth, where mankind would find a temporary home until the fullness of time, when Jesus would redeem, restore, and perfect us through the shedding of His own blood.

God declares a truth that cannot be altered: "The wage of sin is death."[47] In other words, if a person commits a single sin, they are sinners and cannot enter the perfection of Heaven but are doomed to eternal separation from God. They must die apart from God and never enter Heaven.

---

[46] Revelations 21:27.
[47] Romans 6:23.

Jesus knew at the moment of God's decision to create man with the ability to make choices that every single person would ultimately make decisions to disobey God, whether it was lying, cheating, stealing, or simply withholding good from someone. We all know we have sinned at least once — if not once a day!

Thus, we are all in a terrible predicament. A single sin means we are barred from Heaven and living in eternity in the presence of God. And, no amount of good deeds going forward can change the fact that we sinned or alter God's nature that requires that the punishment for a single sin is eternal separation from God.

The only remedy is payment of the death penalty by a substitute. Only a human who had never sinned could take the punishment for another and freely give of their own life in exchange. But, there are none. So, for man, that solves nothing, for all have sinned and fallen short of the glory of God.

No matter how much a parent loves you or offers to take your punishment, they cannot, because they, too, are on death row. That's why, before the creation of the world, God the Father and God the Son had to agree that Jesus would leave heaven and take the form of a man.

Now you can see why Jesus had to come to earth. It was not to show you how to live a good life — although Christ Jesus certainly did that — but for the direct purpose of living a sinless human life so He could be the

sinless sacrifice to take the punishment for the guilty —
you and me.

The good news is that, because Jesus was God and
man at the same time, He never sinned.[48] He never lied to
his parents, never stole, and never cheated. He endured
every temptation, but never sinned. If He had, we would
not have a Savior, because only the innocent lamb could
pay the penalty for the guilty.

You can see where this is going. Only God Himself
could live a sinless human life. Only Jesus, after taking
the form of a man, could do that. Only Jesus would be
willing and able to take the punishment that His creation
deserved.

That's why, thousands of years ago, at the moment of
creation of mankind, the Triune God had a conversation
about whether to create humans in the first place. It was
because Jesus had to agree that He would take the form
of a man, be tempted, yet live a sinless life and willingly
die on a cross for the sins of all mankind.[49] It was on that
day that Jesus agreed to be a gift to man — a gift to you!

The good news is that, two thousand years ago, He
fulfilled that promise! Jesus, indeed, came down from
heaven to take the form of a man in order to fulfill the
pledge He made at the moment of creation: That He
would dwell among man in order to redeem and restore

---

[48] 2 Corinthians 5:21.
[49] John 3:16 ("For God so loved the world that He gave His one and only
Son, that whoever believes in Him shall not perish but have eternal life.").

man and pay the price for the gift that God the Father gave to Jesus. Jesus willingly laid down His life for you!

How do you accept this free, life-saving gift? The Bible says, "If we confess our sins, He is faithful and just and will forgive us our sins and purify us from all unrighteousness."[50] To all who receive Jesus, to those who believe in Him, He gives the right to become children of God and therefore inherit eternal life together with God in heaven.[51]

But, just like every other gift, the receiver must accept the gift. That means you must personally accept the free gift of forgiveness. The good news is that, if you turn to Jesus, allow Him to wash you in His perfect holiness, and accept His shed blood as a sacrifice for your sins, you will no longer be considered impure, no matter what bad things you've ever done or will do.

Accepting the Gift and Dedication to Jesus

It's time to accept Jesus as a gift. It's time for you to make Jesus Lord and Master of your life.

Right now, go to God with a surrendered heart, and receive the gift of Jesus. You'll be asking Jesus, who paid your death penalty, not only to forgive you for going your own way, but to enter and forever own your heart. You'll be giving Jesus permission and control. You'll

---

[50] 1 John 1:9.
[51] John 1:12.

be agreeing to become a willing, obedient child. Pray something like this:

> *God the Father, I know that I am a sinner and deserve death. I know that Your Son, Jesus, is also God and that He came to earth to die on the cross to rescue me from the penalty of my sin. Please forgive me. I receive the free gift of eternal life, which comes solely from the perfect sacrifice of Jesus Christ for my sin. I pray and ask You, Jesus, to come into my heart right now and to make it Your permanent home. Take total control of my life. I choose to follow You and turn away from sin, including my former lifestyle. I also invite God the Holy Spirit to be my life Guide, convict my heart of pride, and keep pointing me back to You whenever I stray. Thank You, God, three in one, for loving me and forgiving me. I commit to following You forever. In the precious name of Jesus I pray these things. Amen.*

If you prayed this prayer with your heart, then congratulations! You're free from the power of sin and death. Both Jesus and the Holy Spirit now permanently live in you. You're now and will forever be God's child. Every name and promise mentioned in this book and God's Book are forever yours. The power of God is available to you when you yield your entire life to Jesus.

Now, the journey begins — but you'll never travel alone again!

A wonderful by-product of having an intimate relationship with God is victory over all sins. Jesus desires to take control of your life and lead you in His holy and pure ways. The power of the Holy Spirit is ready, willing, and more than able to lead you victoriously if you let Him, but you must want to love and serve God more than your former selfish and prideful ways. You need to start turning away from all things that interfere with your daily relationship with Jesus or following God.

The next and final chapter guides you in your journey of purposing to daily become a gift back to Jesus.

Modern-Day Psalm: The Gift of Jesus

What a precious gift of Jesus — a gift to all mankind.
At what great cost and yet given so free!

How magnificent is the Lord Jesus and worthy of praise.
He lifts up the downtrodden and renews the weary.

There is none He turns away. All who seek will find.
Each person is precious in His sight.

When we are weak, He is strong.
He gives rest to those who call upon His name.

Drop to your knees, all who would be set free.
Open your eyes to the wonders of His glory.
Turn away from darkness and into the light.
Seek cleansing and healing.
Renew your faith in the Faithful One.
He alone saves. He alone gives life.

How magnificent is the Lord.
Praise His Holy Name and worship His majesty.
Place your sole trust in Him.

Riches rot and human efforts fail, but the Lord
is above all.
Nothing can separate us from His love.
No distance is too far for Him to reach.

Leap for joy that you are called "chosen."
All sins are freely forgiven.
Attend His banquet, and enter His throne.
Leave the world behind and enter His rest.
Then you shall rejoice. Then you shall see His
face.
For you have been offered the precious gift of
Jesus.

Chapter 6
Gift Back to Jesus

Jenny kissed Bessie and whispered to her, "Happy birthday. You are one year old, a big girl now. I love you!"

IT WAS A MATCH MADE IN HEAVEN. The two were inseparable. Jenny spent nearly every waking moment that she could with Bessie. They even slept together at night.

When they were apart, both constantly longed to be together again. Jenny had tons of pictures of Bessie on her phone. She would flip through them and recall fond memories, filling the time until they could reunite.

Bessie missed Jenny just as much. When Jenny went to school, Bessie perched on the couch so she could see out the window and watch for Jenny to come home. She remained attentive all day long.

Bessie's ears would perk up when she heard the bus coming up the hill nearly a mile away. As it got closer, she would bark and fetch Jenny's mom, herding her to the door, and even grab the leash in her mouth so they could go outside to wait at the bus stop.

"Okay, okay, Bessie, I'm coming. We'll go get Jenny. I know you've missed her."

The greeting at the bus stop was the same each day. Being an Australian Shepherd without a tail, Bessie would wiggle her entire backside when she got excited. She would spin in circles and bark as Jenny got off the bus and then jump up into her arms. The two of them would race home to play their daily game of catch.

To avoid wasting time going into the house, Jenny kept the Frisbee in her school backpack. As soon as they reached the yard, she would yell, "Ready?"

Bessie would take off as fast as she could. As far as Jenny could throw it, Bessie would race to catch the Frisbee in mid-air, only to hurry back to drop it off at Jenny's feet and then turn and take off for another catch. Only when Jenny's arm got tired did the game end, and they would finally go inside for a well-deserved snack as they read a book together.

Bessie longed to please Jenny and would do anything she asked. She was a great friend and loyal companion.

Jenny's mom had told her when she first got her puppy, "If you spend one year training your dog, you will have a well-trained dog for life."

Jenny took that seriously and spent hours a day training Bessie. All their hard work paid off. Now, Bessie understood more than two-dozen commands. If Jenny raised her right hand high, Bessie would lie down. A circle motion meant to roll over. One of Jenny's favorite tricks was to point a finger and say "bang." Bessie would dramatically fall down like a Hollywood actress, lie on her back, and play dead.

Two Greatest Commands
Dogs can be a great example for humans. They get excited when greeting their masters, they long to obey, and simply love to spend time with their master.

As children of God, we love Jesus, our Master. Deep down, we want to please Him. But, we don't instantly know everything to do. We sometimes need discipline or correction, and if we are honest, some commands are harder than others to obey.

When we were young in our faith, God started out small with us, with two simple commands.

Love God, your master, with all of your heart.
Love others.[52]

Jesus tells us that the entire Bible is summed up with these two commands.[53] That's the beauty of the simple Gospel of Jesus.

[52] Matthew 22:36–39.
[53] Ibid.

We need to practice getting these two commands right so that we can better understand and appreciate the other commands that build on them in order to please our Master. As we grow in faith of Jesus, our Lord, we can handle more commands without being overwhelmed.

A good dog is obedient, friendly, patient, confident, and gentle. By comparison, the characteristic of a child of God is love, joy, peace, forbearance, kindness, goodness, faithfulness, gentleness, and self-control.[54] These don't come easily. They require a lot of practice. To learn these qualities, we must spend a lot of time in training with our Master, just like Bessie did.

Of all these traits of a good dog, one of the greatest is obedience. If Bessie never obeyed a command to sit, stay, or come, she would likely run away, get lost, or worse yet, be hit by a car.

Like humans, not every dog is born with a desire to obey commands.

In our family, we once knew a stubborn, self-willed dog named Belle. Actually, it was our good friend's dog that lived a few doors down, but we loved her as our own. Because she was at our house so much, we jokingly claimed coownership — or at least godparent-visitation rights.

Belle was an Australian Shepherd, just like Bessie. But, unlike Bessie, Belle could not help herself when there was a deer or squirrel anywhere in the neighborhood. If

---

[54] Galatians 5:22–23.

she could get off the leash or fly through an open door, she took off. It might be thirty minutes or three hours before she would wander home, exhausted and muddy. Each time she got away, we would receive a neighborhood alert or an all-points bulletin for a search-and-rescue operation. We spent many hours combing the woods, calling out for Belle.

Those were some scary days. But, that's not the worst of it. We knew that Belle needed some serious training after she broke my wife's wrist. On a walk one day, she pulled so hard on the leash to chase a squirrel that Theresa was thrown to the ground. It was not the first broken bone caused by Belle's single-mindedness. She once broke her owner's ribs by pulling her into a tree! There were other sprains and injuries to various parties who had innocently tried to hang onto the leash when Belle went crazy.

One summer, we had three weeks' custody of Belle because her owners had weddings, vacations, and FCA camp to attend. On this occasion, we perhaps took our "coownership" claim a bit too far. In our hearts, we knew that we either had to stop walking Belle, which is the worst thing you can do for a herding dog with a high energy level, or give her some serious training. That's the summer I bought a shock collar. Please let me finish the story before you call PETA.

We live on an acre of land that backs up to a two hundred acre park. That means we have deer and squirrels constantly in our yard. Belle had escaped more than once to give chase. We knew we simply needed to allow Belle more freedom than a ten-foot leash allowed.

On that momentous day, we put flags marking the boundary of our backyard and walked Belle around the perimeter. We gave her some instructions, knowing she would figure out what was happening on her own in due time. We put the shock collar on and took off the leash.

As expected, Belle booked it for the woods. After giving the oral command, "Belle, come," followed by hitting the "beep" button for her new collar, we pressed the "shock" mode. We nearly cried when Belle yelped. But, she stopped in her tracks not knowing what the heck had just happened. She raced home to our loving cries, "Belle, come! Belle, come!" Belle ran to us for security, comfort, and love.

After a few minutes of hugging, we repeated the same process, which had the identical result. But, when she came back, she cocked her head as she stared at the control box in our hands. It was as if a light bulb went on as she figured it out. The next time a deer crossed into the yard, Belle took off in hot pursuit. But, for the first time in her life, she obeyed the beep and our "Belle, come" command. She actually stopped in her tracks at the flag line as the deer bounded away. No shock button required!

Belle proudly pranced back as if to say, "Aren't you proud of me?" Yes, we were, and we sure praised her.

Because we set a boundary for Belle, she was able to have the same thrill of the chase and do what herding dogs do, but within a safety zone. She could have both her sprinting and patrolling duties every day, not only like in the past when she was disobedient and figured out how to sneak away.

Belle loved her freedom so much that we began buying bags of corn and other food for deer and squirrels as bribes to keep inviting them into the yard to help us keep training Belle. The critters were all too willing. Over the next three weeks, we had a dozen deer and even more squirrels visiting almost hourly. We would open the back door anytime Belle whined and wanted to give chase. Remarkably, Belle would almost always stop right at the flag line. It only took a few more times of correction, and Belle not only never ran away again but never ran past the yard line!

The deer seemed quite content, too. It turned into a big game to both of them, like "Capture the Flag" is to your kids. The deer knew that Belle would not cross into the woods, but the food was twenty yards inside the yard. Hours upon hours a day, they played the game. Sometimes the deer could eat for an hour before Belle announced, "Here I come!" She barked and whined as the door swung open. (We even put a cow's bell on the door to give the deer more advance notice, as if they needed it!)

What joy we had sitting outside for hours on Saturdays hanging out with Belle and watching the deer or squirrels play the game. Belle would be so tired by the afternoon that the deer would hardly pay her any attention until Belle could muster the energy to ask her tired muscles to give a half-hearted chase.

After that, Belle gained her freedom from training. We've never needed to use that shock collar again. Belle now gets all her herding-exercise needs through bursts of racing to the tree line; something she never got on a leash. Belle can even go on walks in the woods, and she never strays far. Gone also are the days of worry that she will get run over by a car! (And, yes, the real owners did forgive us for not asking for permission to train their dog in this manner.)

Humans need training, too. We don't always know the dangers around the corner that our Master sees. We don't always understand why He gives us certain commands, but we need to trust that He knows and has our best interests in His heart.

Just as Bessie proved her love for Jenny by obeying and Belle proved her love for us, we can prove our love for Jesus by obeying. In fact, Jesus says that to love Him is to obey His commands.[55]

The good news is that, deep inside, we long to please Jesus. We want to give back to the one who loved us so much that He willingly was crucified on a cross to pay for our punishment.

---

[55] John 14:15, 23.

But, it isn't that easy. We sometimes focus so much upon ourselves or our circumstances that we can't see Jesus, even though He is always right there with us! At other times, we get stubborn, and we may need a shock collar or at least be disciplined by our Master.

Although discipline doesn't feel good at the time, when God disciplines, it has a divine purpose. In fact, it isn't a form of punishment or rejection. Here's how the Bible describes it:

> God disciplines us for our good, in order that we may share in His holiness. No discipline seems pleasant at the time, but painful. Later on, however, it produces a harvest of righteousness and peace for those who have been trained by it.[56]

We don't always know that we can get hurt by things unseen, just as Belle didn't understand the dangers of running across a road. Yet, it's out of love that Jesus disciplines and trains us. Here's another way the Bible describes our need for and purpose of discipline:

> And have you completely forgotten this word of encouragement that addresses you as a father addresses his son? It says, 'My son, do not make light of the Lord's discipline,

---

[56] Hebrews 12:10–11.

and do not lose heart when he rebukes you,
because the Lord disciplines the one he
loves, and he chastens everyone he accepts
as his son.' Endure hardship as discipline;
God is treating you as his children. For what
children are not disciplined by their father?[57]

Where does this leave us? The point is that we need
to start seeing God as good. Even in the midst of trials,
God is good. As we correct our backwards thinking about
discipline and God's perfect love, we start seeing the
true nature of God and begin appreciating His perfect
character.

As we turn the focus off ourselves and put it onto
God, we start realizing that God never left us and never
forsook us. We accept that He was right there with us;
that He paid the penalty for us; and that He loves us
unconditionally and freely forgives. Now we can begin
to see Him as He really is: Good.

Once you see God as good, you'll want to obey, just
as Bessie longed to obey her loving, kind master. But
more than just doing good deeds, you'll want to spend
time with your loving, kind master, Jesus Christ.

Be a Gift Back to Jesus

We've come full circle now. God the Father gave you
as a precious gift to His only son, Jesus. Jesus was

---

[57] Hebrews 12:5–7.

thrilled to receive you — so much so that He not only gave you His name but hundreds of promises and even His very life.

Nothing can separate you from the love of Jesus. He paid the ultimate price for your freedom so you will be with Him in heaven for all eternity and are now free to enjoy divine unity on earth.

What's your response to this perfect and unconditional love? Do you feel compelled to give your life back as a gift to Jesus? Each new day you can purpose and plan to be a gift back to Jesus, the giver of life. Plan to start each day with the same prayer,

> *Good morning, Lord. Today, Jesus, I live for you, with you, and through you. I am your willing, obedient servant. You are mine, and I am yours. I will talk to you throughout the day. I will look for you in everything. I will make time to bless others so that they will know that you love them, too.*

Plan to be a gift to Jesus by spending each moment of each day thinking about, talking to, and just being with your heavenly master, savior, and friend, Jesus Christ. After all, the Gospel of Jesus is summed up in the title of this book. That title is about you: *You are God's Gift to Jesus.*

Pay It Forward

As you embrace gift giving the way God intended, you'll not only fall head-over-heels in love with Jesus, but you'll also want to bless others with the same blessings God has given you. In fact, the innate need for gift giving is so strongly implanted in us that a movie and organizations have been named *Pay It Forward*, based upon the premise that, if you've been the beneficiary of a good deed, you should pass it on to others.

God's circle and cycle of gift giving is the true genesis of paying it forward. Because God first gave you four divine gifts, you have been the beneficiary of blessings that cannot be repaid to the original benefactor. But the beauty of God's gifts is that they are given from pure, unselfish motives of blessing you because He loves you unconditionally and fully. As you receive and enjoy these good gifts, you become the obedient, grateful, thankful, and content son or daughter of Jesus that you were destined to become. Next, because God made all other humans in His image and loves them, too, it becomes almost automatic to want to bless others as the joy of gift giving becomes your new and permanent nature.

Concluding Encouragement

Let me leave you with one final encouragement. One of the greatest first gifts you might give to others is sharing the good news about God's gifts with your family and friends. Purchase or lend them a copy of this book, and start a discussion with them about gift giving and the ultimate gift giver. You'll soon find that gift giving is contagious and more rewarding than you could ever have imagined. After all, we are created in the image of the ultimate gift giver. Therefore, make it your mission to get to know God, enjoy His gifts, and share Him with others!

Modern-Day Psalm: A Gift Back to Jesus

Where is your passion?
Arise from your slumber.
The Lord is risen!
He has come to rule the earth.
Come meet Him in the courtyard.
Hear the words He has to say.

Rise up, Oh Man of God.
The time is here.
Make ready your heart, and open your ears.
He has summoned you by name.
Greet Him with a holy kiss, and pledge your
undying allegiance.

All hail the King.
Praise His mighty name.
Honor His deeds of valor.

Quicken your pace.
Run to His side.
Crown Him with your faithful obedience.

Make ready for battle.
Rid your heart of idols.
He has come for you.
He commands you to carry his staff.

He presents you with His ring.
His robes adorn your frame.

Devote yourself fully.
With passion, praise the Lord.
With passion, take up His cause.
Let praises rule the day.

I answer His call.
I will follow and obey with a glad heart
along the way.
I devote my life fully as a gift back to Jesus.

Appendix

NAMES OF GOD THE FATHER

Abba Father (Romans 8:15)
Ancient of Days (Daniel 7:9, 13)
Creator (Isaiah 27:11)
Father (Luke 11:2)
Father of the Heavenly Lights (James 1:17)
God Almighty (Genesis 17:1–2)
God Most High (Genesis 14:18–22)
God of Abraham, Isaac, and Jacob (Exodus 3:6)
God of Heaven and Earth (Ezra 1:2; 5:11)
God of Hope (Romans 15:13)
God Our Father (Ephesians 1:2)
Holy One (Isaiah 43:15)
Judge of the Earth (Psalm 94:2)
King (Isaiah 43:15)
King of Glory (Psalm 24:7–10)
King of Heaven (Daniel 4:37)
Living God (Romans 9:26)

Lord of All the Earth (Joshua 3:11)
Righteous Father (John 17:25)
The God of All Comfort (2 Corinthians 1:3)
The Great and Awesome God (Nehemiah 1:5)
The Lord Is My Banner (Exodus 17:15)
The Lord Our Maker (Psalm 95:6)
The Lord Who Heals (Exodus 15:26)

NAMES OF GOD THE SON
Advocate (Job 16:19; 1 John 2:1)
Alpha and Omega (Revelation 1:8)
Author and Perfecter (Hebrews 12:2)
Blessed and Only Ruler (Hebrews 2:10)
Bread of God (John 6:33)
Bread of Life (John 6:35)
Bridegroom (Matthew 25:1–10)
Chosen One (Isaiah 41:1)
Christ Jesus Our Lord (2 Timothy 1:2)
Cornerstone (1 Peter 2:6)
Deliverer (Romans 11:26)
Faithful and True (Revelation 19:11)
Foundation (1 Corinthians 3:11)
Fountain (Zechariah 13:1)
Friend (Matthew 11:19)
Gate (John 10:7–9)
Good Shepherd (John 10:11, 14)
High Priest (Hebrews 3:1)
Holy One (Acts 2:27)

Horn of Salvation (Luke 1:69)
I Am (John 8:58)
Immanuel (Matthew 1:23)
King of Kings (1 Timothy 6:14)
Lamb of God (John 1:36)
Light of the World (John 8:12)
Lord of Lords (1 Timothy 6:15)
Master (Matthew 23:8)
Mediator (1 Timothy 2:5)
Messiah (John 1:41)
Mighty God (Isaiah 9:6)
One and Only (John 1:14)
Our Righteousness (1 Corinthians 1:30)
Prince of Peace (Isaiah 9:6)
Redeemer (Isaiah 44:24)
Rock (1 Corinthians 10:4)
Ruler (Matthew 2:6)
Savior (Luke 2:11)
Son of Man (Matthew 8:20)
Sure Foundation (Isaiah 28:16)
Teacher (John 13:14)
The Almighty (Revelation 1:8)
The Beginning (Colossians 1:18)
The Way (John 14:6)
True God (1 John 5:20)
Truth (John 14:6)
Wonderful Counselor (Isaiah 9:6)
Word of God (Revelation 19:13)

NAMES OF GOD THE HOLY SPIRIT

Breath of the Almighty (Job 32:8)

Counselor (John 14:16)

Deposit (Ephesians 1:13–14)

Eternal Spirit (Hebrews 9:14)

Holy Spirit of God (Ephesians 4:30)

Living Water (John 7:38–39)

Promise of the Father (Acts 1:4)

Seal (Ephesians 4:30)

Spirit of Faith (1 Corinthians 12:9)

Spirit of Fire (Isaiah 4:4)

Spirit of God (Genesis 1:2)

Spirit of Judgment (Isaiah 4:4)

Spirit of Knowledge (Isaiah 11:2)

Spirit of Life (Romans 8:2)

Spirit of Power (Isaiah 11:2)

Spirit of Promise (Ephesians 1:13)

Spirit of Truth (John 14:17)

Spirit of Understanding (Isaiah 11:2)

Spirit of Wisdom (Isaiah 11:2)

Spirit Who Intercedes for Us (Romans 8:26–27)

Spirit Who Searches All Things (1 Corinthians 2:10)

GIFT OF YOUR NEW NAMES

Adopted Son / Daughter of God (Ephesians 1:4)
Ambassador of Christ (2 Corinthians 6:3)
Brother to Jesus (Hebrews 2:11)
Child of God (1 John 3:1)
Chosen by God (Colossians 3:12)
Citizen of Heaven (Philippians 3:20)
Dearly Loved (Ephesians 5:1)
Friend of Jesus (John 14:14–15)
Future Judge of Angels (1 Corinthians 6:3)
God's Heir (Galatians 4:7)
God's Holy People (Ephesians 5:31)
God's Possession (Ephesians 1:14)
God's Workmanship (Ephesians 2:10)
Image of God (Genesis 1:27)
Member of God's Household (Ephesians 2:19)
New Creation (2 Corinthians 5:17)
Righteousness of God (2 Corinthians 5:21)
Royal Priest (1 Peter 2:9)
Saint (Psalm 34:9, 85:8)
Salt and Light of the World (Matthew 5:13–14)
Temple of the Holy Spirit (1 Corinthians 6:19)
Wonderfully Created (Psalm 139:14)